Social Media Marketing Guidebook

Social marketing solutions in less than an hour

AMARPREET SINGH

THE THOUGHT FLAME
TURNING SPARK INTO FLAME

info@thethoughtflame.com

www.thethoughtflame.com

Table of Contents

Introduction

When it comes to affiliate marketing, gaining consistent traffic is key to making money online. This is no secret and this is something every good affiliate marketer strives to have on a daily basis so that he or she can make as much money as they want. There is no better way to gain a lot of consistent traffic then by using social media marketing to your advantage.

There are many different kinds of social media platforms that you can use in your affiliate marketing arsenal such as Facebook, Twitter, LinkedIn, Instagram, Reddit and Digg. With the right kind of tactics, online presence and impact you have on your social media networks, you can earn as much endless traffic as you want.

In this eBook you will learn how to market your affiliate marketing campaign with popular social media platforms such as Facebook, Twitter and Reddit so that you can boost the amount of traffic you receive and boost your online sales in the future.

Chapter One: How To Market Effectively On Facebook

Facebook is one of the most popular social media platforms today with over one billion users actively using it worldwide on a daily basis. There are many companies and affiliate marketers that have used Facebook to their advantage by actively marketing on it using certain marketing strategies. In this chapter you will learn how to market on Facebook effectively while becoming a popular online presence on this social media platform.

Effective Facebook Marketing Strategy

In order to market effectively on Facebook, there will be a few steps that you will need to follow in order to make sure you build your presence on the platform without being considered as spam.

Step One: Differentiate Between Whether You Want To Market With Business Pages, Ads or Through Facebook Groups

This will be an important step you will need to follow because every option that is available to you will require you to market it differently. There are many advantages and disadvantages to marketing these different profiles and knowing them will help you determine which we be the best for you to market.

1. Marketing Facebook Pages

Advantages: Pages are free to set up as they can be easily created and accessed through your primary Facebook profile and pages are relatively easy to set up.

Disadvantages: It can be difficult to set up a fan base with a Facebook page. You will need to work hard and consistently to build up a fan base.

2. Marketing Facebook Ads

Advantages: The ads that you create have extremely powerful targeting parameters, which means that you can target whatever size audience you want to target.

Disadvantages: Depending on what your overall goals are, marketing these ads can become quite expensive in the long run.

3. Marketing in Facebook Groups

Advantages: Marketing in Facebook Groups is something that is free to do and groups tend to have high levels on engagement.

Disadvantages: Marketing through this avenue can become very time consuming, which many people are not willing to do.

Marketing With Facebook Pages

As stated above marketing on Facebook through the use of Facebook pages is one of the easiest and simplest ways that you can market on Facebook today. However, it is hard to build a presence on Facebook using this marketing method. If you decide to market as an affiliate market there are many ways that you can make sure that you do it effectively.

1. Customize Your Page Cover Image and Profile Picture

If you have a custom logo that you like to use, you will want to set that up as your main profile picture. It's as simple as that.

Your cover image will be a whole different ball game. You will have to choose for yourself what you will want to use to fill up that space such as money or pictures of the product you are promoting.

2. Fill Out The About Section

This section of your Facebook page is the place where you will want to sell yourself or the product you are promoting to those who visit your page. This is your chance to improve visitors and perhaps even make a couple of sales in the process.

In this section you will want to make sure that you put plenty of good information such as what your company or affiliate program is all about, why your program or company is different from the rest and other important details that you may want to share with your visitors. If you have enough time try to write the About section with your specific targeted audience in mind.

If you have a website or blog this section can be easily created because all that you have to do is copy and paste what you have on your blog straight to this section if you prefer. Regardless of what you decide to do make sure to create this section in a friendly and helpful manner. Whatever you do, do not try to sell your product right off the bat as people are most likely to turn away from your page rather then spend time visiting it. Make it a habit to help people rather than straight up sell to them.

3. Post Helpful and Useful Information To Your Wall On A Daily Basis

If there is one thing most audience's love, it is consistency and relevant information. As such you will want to make it a habit to post relevant and helpful information for your visitors to see on a daily basis. Some of the things that you may want to post regularly can include:

- Links to your blog posts if you have a blog.

- Links to any articles that you may have personally written.

- Coupons or savings codes for the products you are promoting.

- New announcements pertaining to your product or affiliate network.

- Helpful insights that will help your visitors.

4. Do Not Spam Your Wall

If there is one thing that will get you flagged by Facebook as a spam page is by you constantly spamming your wall with posts such as "Buy this now" or "make money online this way." I know that while you are in the game to make money on whatever product you are promoting or by promoting your affiliate network, you will need to resist the urge to spam constantly.

Before posting any new information to your wall, stop and ask yourself if the content you are putting up with me insightful and relevant to what your audience is looking for. If so then post it but if it doesn't, don't risk it. Spamming your wall with useless content will only work to drive your visitors away, not to keep them engaged in what you have to say.

Marketing With Facebook Ads

When it comes to use Facebook ads in your marketing methods, there are several different ads that you can choose from. Each type of ad that you can market with will have different outcomes and will range in price depending on what you need. You can create an ad directly linked to your Facebook Page that you are building an audience for or an ad that will drive traffic directly to your website or blog.

When choosing to market your product or affiliate network with Facebook ads, you will be given the chance to use Facebook's most powerful audience-targeting tool. With this tool you can literally find a large audience to target your ads too based upon whatever you wish.

You can narrow down your audience to specific age, location, what their interests are or even what zip code they are in.

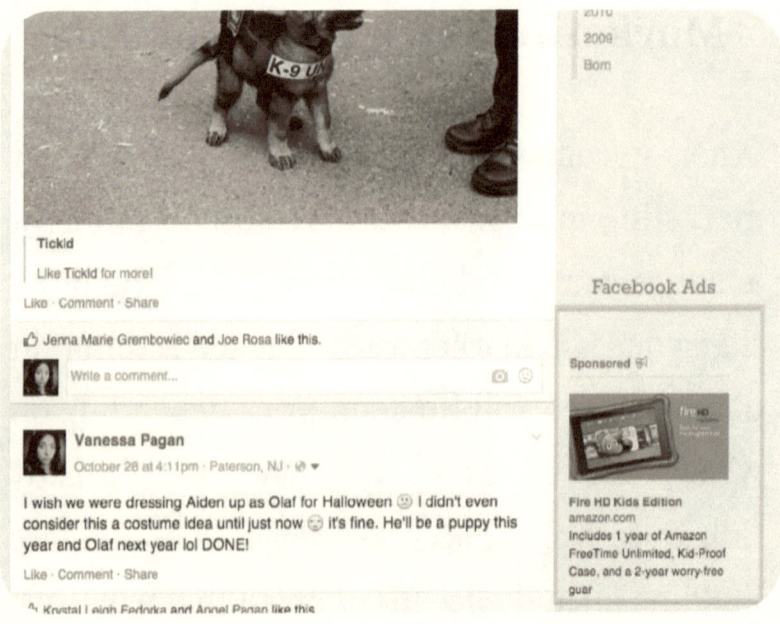

Regardless of the kind of audience you are looking to target, you will be able to customize your Facebook ads according to this audience. Keep in mind that the more ads you have to target different demographic groups, the better results you are going to have.

For example, let's say you want to target baseball fans. If this is your goal it is highly recommend that you create ads for every type of baseball team out there, giving yourself the chance to gain an audience from across the MLB league. Regardless of the kind of ads you wish to create or the specific niche that you want to target, make sure that you take the time to research high quality and relevant keywords to help target your ads accordingly.

Chapter Two: Marketing on Twitter

As of late 2013, Twitter has been estimated to have nearly 53 millions users worldwide that use this social platform on a daily basis. With numbers like this, it makes Twitter one of the most ideal places to market your affiliate product or network. It is such a great place to market that you may be very surprised by how you can utilize the 140 character website to drive a flood of traffic to your sales page on a daily basis.

So, how can you improve your Twitter presence to drive high quality traffic to your sales page and drive more commission payments into your pocket? Here are a few simple tips that you can use to leverage the power of Twitter for your online affiliate business.

1. Make Sure That You Optimize Your Profile On Twitter

To optimize your profile on Twitter effectively, you will want to make sure that both your voice and online presence are branded well together. The best way to do this is to make sure that your bio and tweets have the same kind of voice on a consistent basis and that your tweets reflect what your online affiliate business is all about.

Also make sure that you personalize your bio by adding a link to your sales page or website and giving a clear explanation about who you are and what your company is all about.

2. Make Sure To Communicate With Those Who Are Considered Experts In Your Niche On Twitter and Learn From Them

There is nothing better than learning from those who are already successfully marketing on Twitter. While Twitter itself can seem like a massive platform so finding these experts can become a small challenge. However, to make this task easier simply use the search tool and search for high quality and relevant keywords in your niche and you will be able to narrow down popular users in that particular area.

As soon as you find these users I highly recommend that you begin communicating with them on a daily basis and follow them.

They may post tweets once in a while that you will find extremely helpful and may want to implement into your own marketing campaign.

3. Tweet As Regularly As Possible

Similar to Facebook marketing, the key to success is to post on a consistent and regular basis. Tweeting as often as possible is the sign of an active profile and this is something that followers look for. When posting tweets to your profile, make sure that they are relevant to your niche, high quality content that you know your followers will click on and is content that will get a bunch of retweets.

Consistency is key to be a successful Twitter marketer. Tweeting only once a week or once a month will do nothing but guarantee that you fail in this marketing venture. You want to make sure that you stay on top of your followers minds instead of them just forgetting about you.

4. Regularly Favorite Tweets and Retweet As Often As You Can

If you want to catch the eye of potential followers, then do not be afraid to favorite a tweet or retweet something they have posted. Retweeting is a great way to help you link to relevant posts within the industry and can even go a long way

in helping to showcase you as a leader in the field.

Favoriting tweets on the other hand have more power and pull on audiences as this is something that many marketers are not aware of when they first begin marketing on Twitter. This will immediately get you noticed on Twitter by your followers and can even help you gain more followers in the long run.

5. Follow The Latest Trends and Hashtags As Often As Possible

There is a specific section within Twitter where you can see exactly what is trending on Twitter in real time. Following this real time trends will give you the chance to make connections with the accounts that are trending so that you can make your brand stand out.

My recommendation is to tweet relevant tweets alongside the trending topics as people will see your tweet whenever they search for a specific hashtag. When you tag your tweets with relevant hashtags, you'll give yourself the chance to gain new followers. However, make sure that you use them only sparingly as people may consider it as spam if they are attached to content that is completely irrelevant.

6. Take Advantage of Promoted Tweets

Not sure what promoted tweets are? Well, they are tweets that you ordinarily create and then pay a certain amount to promote it to a specific target audience. Taking advantage of this promotion within Twitter is a great way to target an audience of your choice. However, in order to make sure you get the most out of your promoted tweets make sure that you do not tweet anything that may be considered too spammy or a tweet that tricks people to click on a link.

Remember, keep your tweets fresh and try not to let any tweets that you promote to run for a long period of time. Keep it short and simple and you'll be able to attract new followers to your account.

7. Don't Forget To Use Images and Videos To Your Advantage

Whenever you use images or videos, you will be driving even more traffic to your sales page or website. It has been shown that by using videos and images, affiliate marketers are able to gain at least 3 to 4 times more clicks on their links than marketers who don't utilize them.

You will begin to notice that after a while, plain tweets are just that: plain. While you may be engaging your followers with relevant and insightful content, it will begin to get boring after a while. Adding images and videos to your current tweets will give them richer quality which has been proven to have your followers interact with you more often and will reduce the risk of you receiving negative feedback or comments.

Chapter Three: The Power of Reddit

While many people know of Facebook and Twitter and assume that those are the most powerful social media networking websites online today, many people are unfamiliar with Reddit. As an active and daily user on Reddit myself, I can testify to how effective this social media website is from a marketing standpoint.

If you are not sure what Reddit is, it is simply a social media networking site where users can submit links to picture or websites with other members of the community to share it with. If used correctly you can gain a lot of traffic from Reddit. In order to do it correctly you will need to learn how to market, without marketing. Confusing, I know but this is something you will need to learn and you will need to learn it fast.

The thing is when it comes to using Reddit as a source of marketing, the website has one rule that most marketers have a problem adhering to: No self-promotion. This can be especially tricky if you want to gain traffic to a website or sales page, but just because it is tricky that does not mean it is impossible to do.

Here are a few tips and tricks that you can use to utilize Reddit and to drive lots of traffic to your product sales page or affiliate network page.

Tips To Marketing Successfully On Reddit

1. Build Up Your Karma

Your karma standing on Reddit will give users an idea of how active you are within the community. There are several ways that you can build up your karma such as commenting on other posts, upvoting posts and sharing good links with others in the community. While this may not necessarily increase the ranking of the posts that you share compared to a member who just recently joined, it will go a long way in helping you to improve your status among other "Redditors."

2. Use The Sub-Reddits As Wisely As Possible

When it comes to finding areas within Reddit to post in that fits nicely within your niche, you will need to learn how to use the sub-reddit section. However, there have been times where even I have found the subreddit section to be a tad bit more targeted than I would like. You can find a subreddit category in practically every niche whether it is gaming, copywriting or politics. The key is narrowing down the categories to fit into your needs.

Do your research ahead of time and spend some time going through all of the subreddits to narrow down the ones that will best fit into your needs and that will help drive a lot of traffic to your sales page or website.

3. Post Unique Stories or Links Only

The one reason why many people continue going to Reddit on a daily basis is to find unique, hilarious, cute or inspiring stories or pictures from other users. Remember, this site is a sharing website and the more funny and unique things that you share on it, the more popular you will become on it.

As a user myself I can tell you that I could spend hours on Reddit just looking for things to click on. Can you see where this can come in handy as an affiliate marketer? If you post great content and links to the site and other users like what you post, the more upvotes you will gain and the higher up your link will appear on the website.

Conclusion

There are many different ways to market as an affiliate marketer on social media websites like Facebook, Twitter and Reddit that if I were to write about them all, this book would be well over one hundred pages long. The possibilities are endless and there is a ton of traffic that can be generated from these websites.

However, the important thing to remember with these websites is that you first need to build up an online presence in order to gain the trust of your potential clients. It is also important that you gain the trust of your followers first before trying to sell to them. When you work towards helping your customers first, commission payments will only be shortly behind.

Take the tips and tricks outlined in this eBook and work on building your online presence on a daily basis on the social media websites of your choice and you will soon be on the way to becoming a top earning affiliate marketer.

About Us

The Thought Flame is committed to add value to its customers through various books, online courses and other resources. You can learn more about us and our books at www.thethoughtflame.com.

Don't forget to check out our amazing **online video courses** at www.thethoughtflame.com/courses/ to take your knowledge to another level.

To check out our **extraordinary collection of diet/cookbooks**, visit http://www.thethoughtflame.com/category/non-fictional/cookbooks/ .

As a part of our valued relationship with our customers, we keep providing you free promotional books, courses and other stuff on subscribing with us on our site. We have a strict anti-spam policy and assure you no spam mails will be sent to your mailbox.

To subscribe with us, visit www.thethoughtflame.com.

Like our work and would like to say thanks?

Buy us a cup of coffee at www.thethoughtflame.com/coffee/

<u>Author</u>

Amarpreet Singh is an avid learner and his passion for education has made him travel, work and study all across the world. He holds three masters degrees, including MBA, from top universities in Asia.

He is author of dozens of books, many of which are Amazon's bestseller, varying in various topics and categories. He also teaches many online courses having thousands of students across the world.

He has a keen interest in international affairs, economics, global poverty and politics, financial markets and entrepreneurship, and strives to be part of a community that shares the same passion.

He has worked as consultant with organizations like Airbus and The World Bank. He loves travelling and learning about new cultures, and has been fortunate to live/work/travel/study in countries like India, China, Korea, US, South Africa, Japan, Philippines, Singapore, Canada etc., and learn about the culture and lifestyle in each of them. To check out more of his work, visit www.thethoughtflame.com

www.ingramcontent.com/pod-product-compliance
Lightning Source LLC
Chambersburg PA
CBHW030704190526
45164CB00004B/440